WELCOME! We hope you enjoy this Fave Art-13 album collection of Classis Nude Art (Statues & Paintings). Most art works are copied from the internet, posters, pictures and books. Most are collector's items and can be seen in famous galleries and private homes. The originals are very expensive but copies are available from some dealers. You may display this book as coffee table book in your living room, as conversation piece. You may give this as gift. You may cut out and frame each page. Each art work is 8.5x11 inches and suitable for framing, and for wall decors.

The ISBN Code Numbers of this book are:
ISBN-13: 978- 1547179671 & ISBN-10: 1547179678
Printed in USA. Free to copy by anybody. Why copy? Just buy the book.
My other books list can be accessed at:
http://tinyurl.com/mj76ccq & http://www.jobelizes6.wix.com/mysite.
My contact email is job_elizes@yahoo.com. (Tatay Jobo Elizes, Pub.)

Marble Statue of the Three Graces. Greek

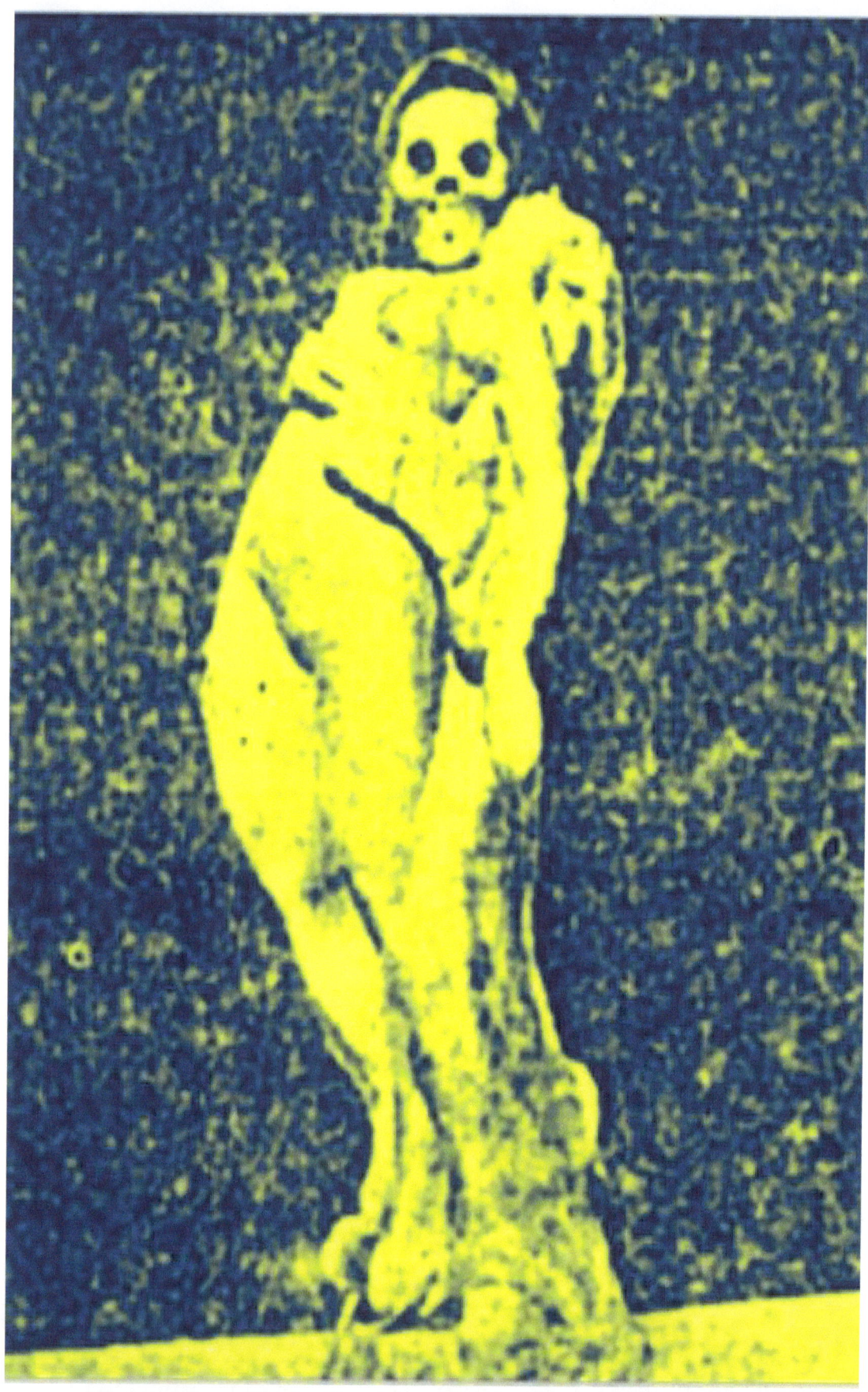

Victory over life by Dr. Jose Rizal, gift to Dr. Blunebtritt

Statue in Rome by Emilio Fiaschi, 1858-1941

By Emilio fiaschi, marble

A.Santini, nude bathing

A.Santini

The Kiss, E. Rodin, 1886

The three graces, 1913, Antonio Canova

Nude, by Matisse, early 1900s

Greek Nude statue

Greek Nude Art

Greek Nude Art

Discobolos, the discus thrower

Aphrodite or Lety's Venus

1575, by Paolo Geronese, early renaissance painting

WELCOME! We hope you enjoy this Fave Art-13 album collection of Classis Nude Art (Statues & Paintings). Most art works are copied from the internet, posters, pictures and books. Most are collector's items and can be seen in famous galleries and private homes. The originals are very expensive but copies are available from some dealers. You may display this book as coffee table book in your living room, as conversation piece. You may give this as gift. You may cut out and frame each page. Each art work is 8.5x11 inches and suitable for framing, and for wall decors.

The ISBN Code Numbers of this book are:

ISBN-13: 978- 1547179671 & ISBN-10: 1547179678

Printed in USA. Free to copy by anybody. Why copy? Just buy the book.

My other books list can be accessed at:

http://tinyurl.com/mj76ccq & http://www.jobelizes6.wix.com/mysite.

My contact email is job_elizes@yahoo.com. (Tatay Jobo Elizes, Pub.)

Sleeping Venus, 1630, by Simon Vouet, 1590-1649

Classic, painter unknown

Nude Forniarina, 1518, by Raphael

Giovanni Bellini – Venetian woman

Nude Study, Renaissance

Nude Study, Renaissance

Nude Study, Renaissance

Botecelli

Impressionist, Renaisssance

Eve & Apple

Nude Study, 19th

Reclining Nude by Isodoro Pils, France, 1841

Birth of Venus

Symbolic Portrait by Charles Messara, 19th

Nude by Juan Luna

By Edgar L. Owen, 19th

Classic Nude by B. Kinlog, 20th

Drinking tea by Granger, 19th, phto-fineart

Ladies, by Russler, Austria, 19ᵗʰ

Nude by Nicolai Gregorescu, 19th

Impressinist, 19th

Nude by William Etty, 1787-1847

By Giovanni Boldini, 19th

Reclinig Nude, 19th

Lovely Art, 19th

Nude Study, 19th

Bachante By The Sea, by Camille Corot, 1865

By Edgar L. Owen, 19th

Goddess Diana by Boucher, 1700s

Eve by William Blake, 1810

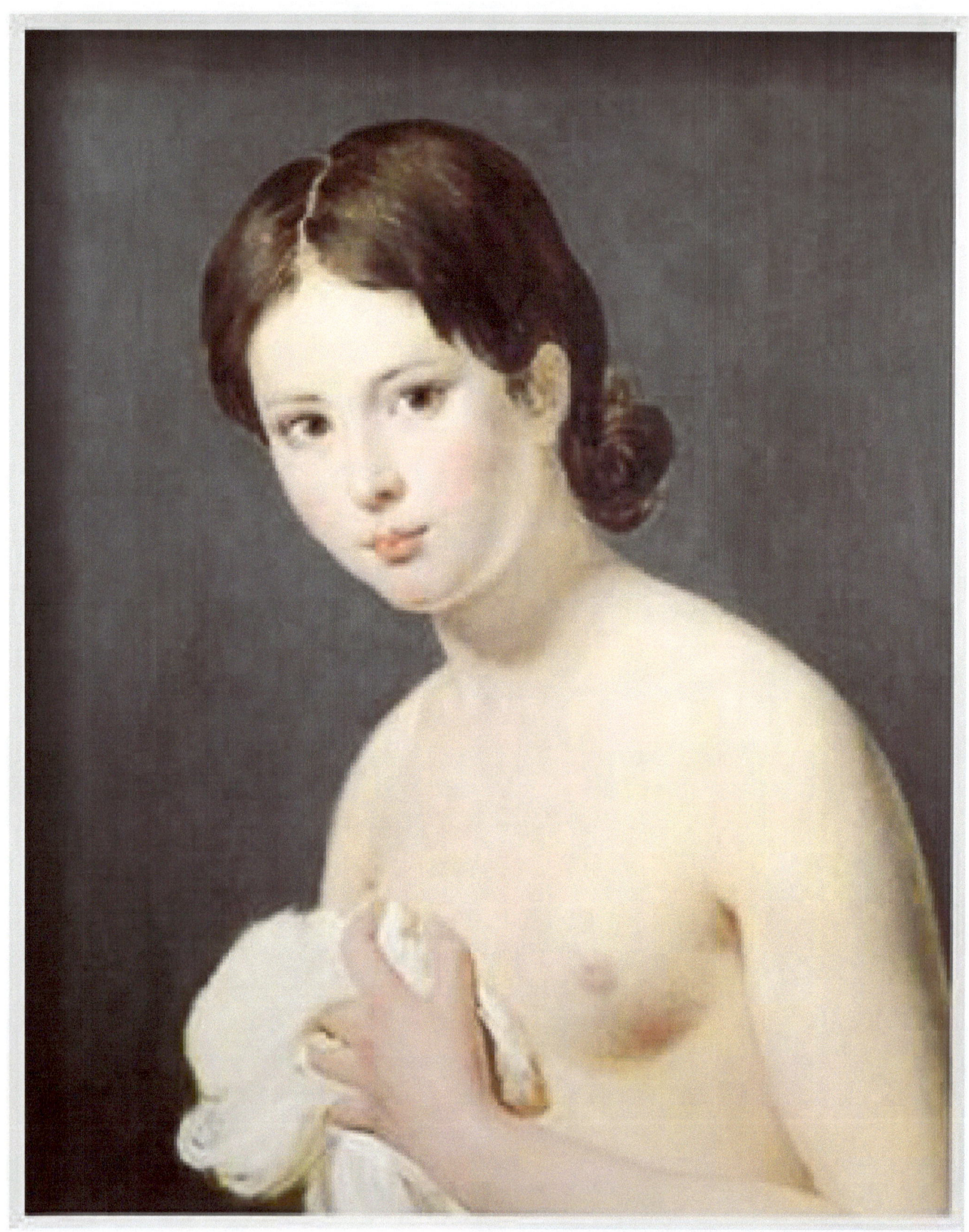

Young Girl by Jacques L. David, 1795

Etude Femme de nue by Charles Joseph Natoire

Stone at cemetery

Modern Painting by Masangkay, courtesy of Edgar O. Cruz, facebook

www.ingramcontent.com/pod-product-compliance
Lightning Source LLC
Chambersburg PA
CBHW051059180526
45172CB00002B/703